They were brought together by the death of her fiancé, his well-loved brother, but from this tragedy was born a deep, if silent, love. The marriage of King George V and Queen Mary reflected their own sober characters and their belief in devotion, respect and, above all, duty.

RAGS TO RICHES

MARRIAGE PROSPECTS FOR AN OBSCURE PRINCESS WITH A FLAWED PEDIGREE SEEMED BLEAK, BUT HER FAIRY GODMOTHER SAW TO IT THAT SHE SHOULD BE TWICE BETROTHED TO THE HEIR TO THE BRITISH THRONE

W HEN PRINCE GEORGE WAS BORN HIS situation was very similar to Prince Harry's today: his grandmother, Queen Victoria, was still on the throne, and he was the second son of the Prince and Princess of Wales, later King Edward VII and Queen Alexandra.

He was born in the early hours of the morning on 3 June 1865 at Marlborough House, London, a month prematurely, and was christened George Frederick Ernest Albert on 7 July 1865.

Georgie was a plump, sturdy little boy, rather different from his lanky and lethargic brother. Edward was a relaxed and indulgent father and Prince George had a glorious early childhood. His mother, too, loved her children more than anything, and although Albert Victor (known as Eddy) was her favourite child, there was plenty of love left over for George, who adored his mother. 'I was brought up in an age of beautiful women,' he would say, 'and the two most beautiful of all were the Empress Elisabeth of Austria and my own mother.'

The autocratic grandmother

Alix's adoration of her children meant she found it impossible to deny them anything. Queen Victoria did not approve. The boys occasionally went to stay with her and she visited them regularly. She watched them keenly and decided they needed formal education.

Eventually Bertie and Alix agreed. In 1871, when George was six years old, a tutor, the Reverend John Neale Dalton, was appointed to teach him and Eddy. A year later the Queen was still not sure whether his teaching had had any effect and she was quite out of patience with their upbringing.

But by 1874 Reverend Dalton was able to send Queen Victoria favourable reports on both his charges, written from the Prince of

👑 *Second in command: little did Prince George* left *know that, inheriting the throne by default, he would, one day, be known as the Sailor King. At his birth* below, *as the second son of Bertie and Alix, then Prince and Princess of Wales, he was only fourth in line to the throne, preceded as he was by his elder brother, the heir apparent, Albert Victor*

Wales's estate in Norfolk: 'The two little Princes ride on ponies for an hour each alternate morning in the week, and take a walk on the other three days. In the afternoon also their Royal Highnesses take exercise on foot. As regards the studies, the writing, reading and arithmetic are all progressing favourably; the music, spelling, English history, Latin, geography, and French all occupy a due share of the Royal Highnesses' attention.' By the time he was 11 George had grown into a healthy, sturdy, handsome boy, although he was rather

By gracious permission of HM the Queen

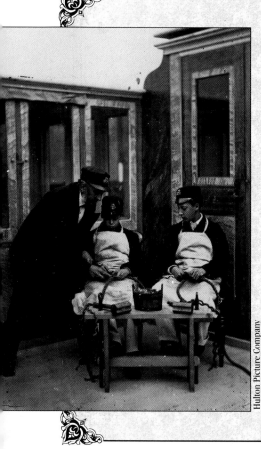

LIFE ON THE OCEAN WAVES

Georgie never forgot the bullying he received at the hands of the other naval cadets on the *Britannia*. He said later that he often wished he hadn't been a prince. 'The other boys made a point of taking it out on us on the grounds that they'd never be able to do it later on,' he remembered. 'There was a lot of fighting among the cadets and the rule was that if challenged you had to accept. So they used to make me go up and challenge the bigger boys – I was awfully small then – and I'd get a hiding time and again . . .' They also used to send him off on illegal errands to buy tuck. He was invariably found out, punished, and the food confiscated: 'The worst of it was, it was always *my* money; they never paid me back – I suppose they thought there was plenty more where that came from, but in point of fact we were only given a shilling a week pocket money.' The worst of the bullying came to an end when one of the bigger boys he was forced to fight punched him on the nose and gave him a severe nose-bleed. 'It was the best blow I ever took,' he said, 'for the Doctor forbade my fighting any more'

Hulton Picture Company

ters very much. 'Please give Victoria my very best love and many kisses, and mind you kiss her properly, like I would if I was there,' he wrote in an agony of homesickness.

Around the world on a warship

In 1879 George and Eddy, their training over, joined the warship *Bacchante*. For three years George travelled the world, treated in almost exactly the same way as his fellow shipmates. He ate the monotonous diet of salt pork and ship's biscuit while at sea, which was only varied by exotic food when they docked in foreign ports. Georgie never did like anything but plain English fare, so neither suited him. One of his best meals was at a state banquet in Japan, where he ate the boiled rice eagerly.

Travel did not give Georgie a taste for foreign lands (in later life he was quoted as saying 'Abroad is awful – I know because I've been there'). He enjoyed few of the countries he visited. One great pleasure was being tattooed in Japan and Jerusalem. His terse summing up of China in his diary read, 'The stinks are something awful!'

Alone for the first time

At the end of these three years George was 17. Life at sea had toughened him, though he never

small for his age. He was altogether a brighter spark than his brother, who was taller but dull and not interested in anything. Next to Eddy, George looked like a positive firebrand. The Reverend Dalton noted in his diary that George had 'fretfulness of temper' and a tendency to 'self-approbation' among his faults.

If Queen Victoria was impressed by the improvement of the Wales's children's behaviour under their tutor it hardly showed. She had other things to complain about. She had turned against Alix not least because she was producing children far less robust than would have suited the autocratic Queen. She thought they were a sickly brood. 'Most wretched,' she wrote of them, 'excepting Georgie, who is always merry and rosy.'

In the Navy

It had long been decided that Georgie should make his career in the Royal Navy, and in 1877 when he was 12 years old he was sent to join the training ship *Britannia* as a naval cadet. It was decided that Prince Eddy, who had been destined for public school, should join Georgie as a naval cadet instead. Without his younger brother around it was feared Eddy would find it impossible to do any work at all and would simply go into a decline.

George wrote long, loving letters to his mother. He missed his home and his young sis-

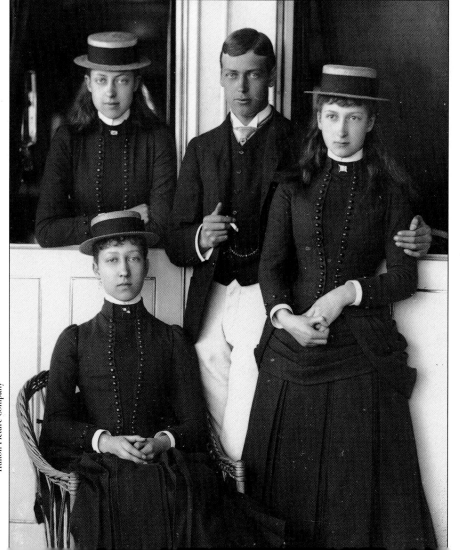

Hulton Picture Company

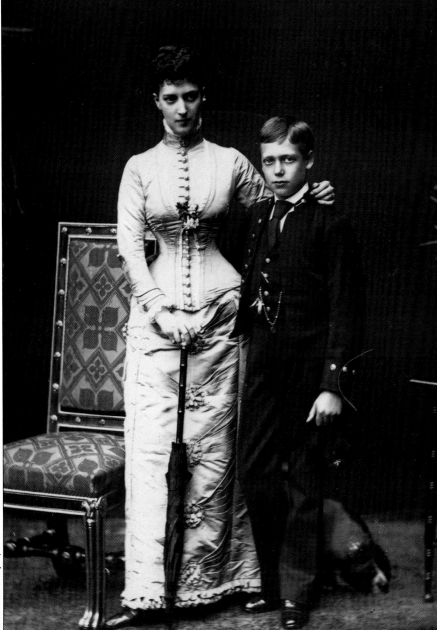

got over his sea-sickness. His first voyage alone, without brother or tutor, was in 1883 and he received his first command in July 1889.

It was a lonely existence. He had been trained to keep his distance from fellow seamen and so continued to be inordinately attached to his family, particularly his mother, to whom he had promised to 'resist all temptation' – by which he meant women. Even so, he fell in love with a granddaughter of Sir Robert Peel, Julie Stonor, but he was not allowed to marry her because she was both a commoner and a Roman Catholic.

Georgie was introduced to a more dissipated life by Eddy. His brother, having shown no interest for anything in life before, had discovered an inordinate enthusiasm for sex.

'It never did me any good

to be a Prince'

GEORGE IN LATER YEARS

Eddy allowed George to share a woman he had set up in a flat in St John's Wood ('She is a ripper,' he wrote in his diary), and then Georgie 'kept' a girl at Southsea.

Having not been allowed to marry the girl he loved, and knowing that he could never marry the sort of girls with whom he had sex, Georgie was perfectly resigned to the idea of an arranged marriage.

♔ *George had doting parents, whom he, in turn, adored, especially Alexandra above. Even as a grown man, he would begin a letter to her, 'My own sweet beloved Motherdear'. And, when he was a bearded naval officer commanding a gunboat, she would write, 'With a great big kiss for your lovely little face'. George was very close to his family, especially his younger sister, Victoria seated left. Two sisters, Louise, the Princess Royal far left, and Maud, who became Queen of Norway right, completed the Wales family, along with their eldest brother, Albert Victor left in picture right, known as Eddy. George could run rings around Eddy, but Alexandra implored him not to irritate the heir to the throne; and, anyway, it was not difficult to keep the peace with a brother so dim and placid; indeed, George ended up protecting him from others*

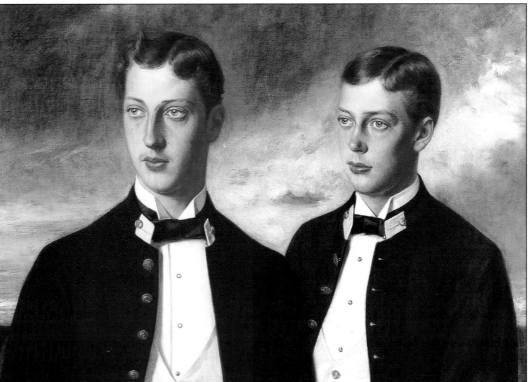

Hulton Picture Company

♛ *The Honourable Julia Stonor above was a childhood friend and George's first love. But as she was a commoner and a Catholic, they could not marry. However, he retained a deep affection for her – she was the only commoner allowed to call him George. In 1891, she married the Marquis de Hautpoul de Seyre*

THE CINDERELLA PRINCESS

Princess May of Teck made an unlikely Cinderella – but that is how her early life has sometimes been described. Certainly by royal standards hers was a rags-to-riches story, not just in terms of wealth but also royal status.

To be born a Princess in Kensington Palace would seem to be a good start in life, but the little girl who came into the world on 26 May 1867 was much to be pitied. Before she had drawn her first breath it was agreed that her marriage prospects were slight. She was too royal to marry a commoner yet not royal enough to marry into royalty.

The problem was her father's side of the family. Prince Francis of Teck was the son of Duke Alexander of Württemberg who had ignored the ladies of royal blood in his circle to contract a morganatic marriage. This meant that Francis was removed from the line of succession to the throne of Württemberg, and was not allowed to use the title of Royal Highness. This put the young Prince Francis in a difficult position himself when it came to marrying a suitable bride. So he was pleasantly surprised when it was suggested that he might pay his suit to the much higher ranking HRH Princess Mary Adelaide of Cambridge.

The good-looking bachelor of 28 soon discovered the snag. Princess Mary was 32 and, frankly, fat. The more eligible men of her generation had not wanted to marry her. But she was a nice person with plenty of money of her own and, if Francis was undecided, Queen Victoria's approval soon made up his mind for him. They were married in Kew Church on 12 June 1866 and moved into apartments in Kensington Palace. Their daughter was born just under a year later, and christened Victoria Mary Augusta Louise Olga Pauline Claudine Agnes. Queen Victoria, who had made the match, was delighted to be godmother to the 'dear, merry, healthy child', even though she was 'not as handsome as she ought to be'.

Her mother soon nicknamed her daughter 'my May-flower', and it was as Princess May that she came to be known. (It was only when her husband eventually came to the throne that she was called Mary.)

The spendthrift Duke and Duchess

The Duke of Teck had never had any money to call his own, but the Duchess was quite well provided for. She received an income of £5000, and her mother matched the sum from

Ties of Duty and Love

George III (1738-1820) m. Charlotte of Mecklenburg-Strelitz (1744-1818)

Victoria, Princess of Saxe-Coburg-Saalfield (1786-1861) m. Edward, Duke of Kent (1767-1820)

Adolphus, Duke of Cambridge (1774-1850) m. Augusta, Princess of Hesse-Cassel (1797-1889)

Albert, Prince of Saxe-Coburg-Gotha (1819-1861) m. Victoria (1819-1901)

Alexandra, Princess of Denmark (1844-1925) m. Edward VII (1841-1910)

Mary Adelaide (1833-1897) m. Francis, Duke of Teck (1837-1900)

Albert Victor, Duke of Clarence (1864-1892)

George V (1865-1936) m. Victoria Mary of Teck (1867-1953)

Edward VIII (1894-1972) | George VI (1895-1952) | Mary (1897-1965) | Henry, Duke of Gloucester (1900-1974) | George, Duke of Kent (1902-1942) | John (1905-1919)

The return to England

In 1885 the family returned to England and White Lodge in Richmond Park, where they settled. May was now given a French governess who taught her social history and about the problems of the industrial society. Her mother, whose lack of funds was partly caused by her generous philanthropic nature, decided that May was now ready to learn her duties towards those less fortunate. Both mother and daughter had a full programme of visiting the sick and distressed – something May did with real warmth and compassion.

Too royal, yet not royal enough

May had now reached marriageable age, but she knew that her morganatic blood was going to make this matter difficult for her. She was a fine-looking girl, but not a beauty or even pretty. She held herself with great dignity and had bright blue eyes, intelligent and enquiring. And, although she was not remotely fat like her mother, her figure was not elegant. She longed for marriage, but she was prepared to concede that she was likely to remain a spinster.

her own personal fortune. That should have been plenty of money for the Tecks to live on, especially as they lived in a grace-and-favour residence. But Francis was extravagant and Mary was fun-loving, and together they egged each other on to spend and spend. At one point they airily accepted a loan of £50,000 from a very rich friend (never repaid) but in spite of that, they still managed to run up debts to tradesmen of £20,000.

This state of affairs could not be allowed to continue. Queen Victoria had lost all patience, as had the creditors. The Tecks were firmly advised to take themselves off abroad, where it was possible to live very much more cheaply without loss of face. As May put it, 'My parents were in Short Street so they had to go abroad to economize.'

Life in Florence

Between 1883 and 1885 they settled in Florence. At first, the 16-year-old May hated this foreign city. She complained that the houses were dirty and uncomfortable and that the people smelled of garlic.

But, unlike Georgie, she did not hold these insular views for long. After a while the beauty of Florence took her over, and it was there that she started to develop her fine appreciation for art, which endured throughout her life. She was already a good student of English, French and German and she now added Italian and history of art, and took up singing and painting.

👑 **Above left:** *Kidding around never came easily to May. Her parents, the Duke and larger-than-life Duchess of Teck had extravagant lifestyles that forced the family to flee England and their creditors. Brought up in this uncertain household between two brothers, Adolphus and Francis (Alexander, born last, is not in the picture), May acquired an early gravitas, her life-long hallmark* above. *By the time she was a young woman* right *she had acquired plenty of common sense and good taste which endeared her to Queen Victoria as a suitable future Queen – first, as a bride for the heir apparent, the dissolute Eddy, and later his more suitable younger brother, George*

Family

♛ A sombre portrait of George *right* – an otherwise merry young boy whose nickname was 'the Right Royal Pickle'

George

♛ *Below* George at 17, looking tanned and healthy after three years at sea with the Royal Navy

♛ On board the Royal yacht *Osborne* during Cowes week 1880. *From left to right* Maud, Victoria, Eddy, Alexandra, Edward, George and *in front* Louise

May

♛ Six-year-old May in conversation with a feathered friend *left*

♛ *Below* Three-year-old May, her mother's darling, has a reading lesson

♛ *Left* A scowling May clutches her doll, while younger brothers Francis (in the pram) and Adolphus look on, 1870

May's 'coming-out' gown *below* was a charming combination of white satin and layers of tulle, worn with a beaded headdress of feathers

Popperfoto

Velvet bow trim at shoulder with decorative brooch
Lace-up detail at front of v-shaped bodice
Decorative velvet ribbons and bows hang from below the waist
Hand painted paper folding fan

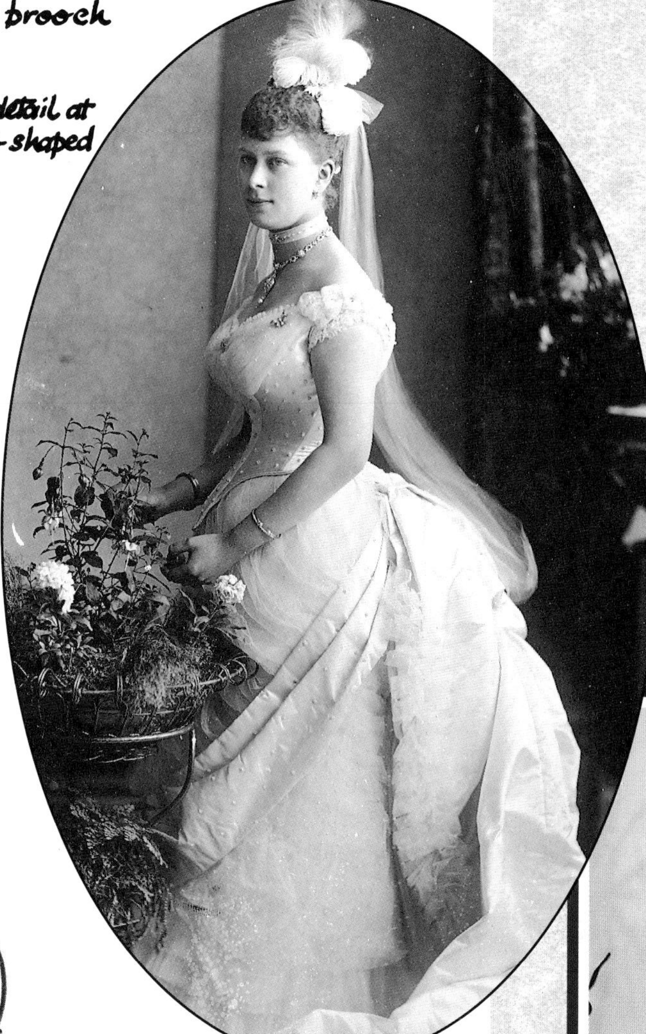

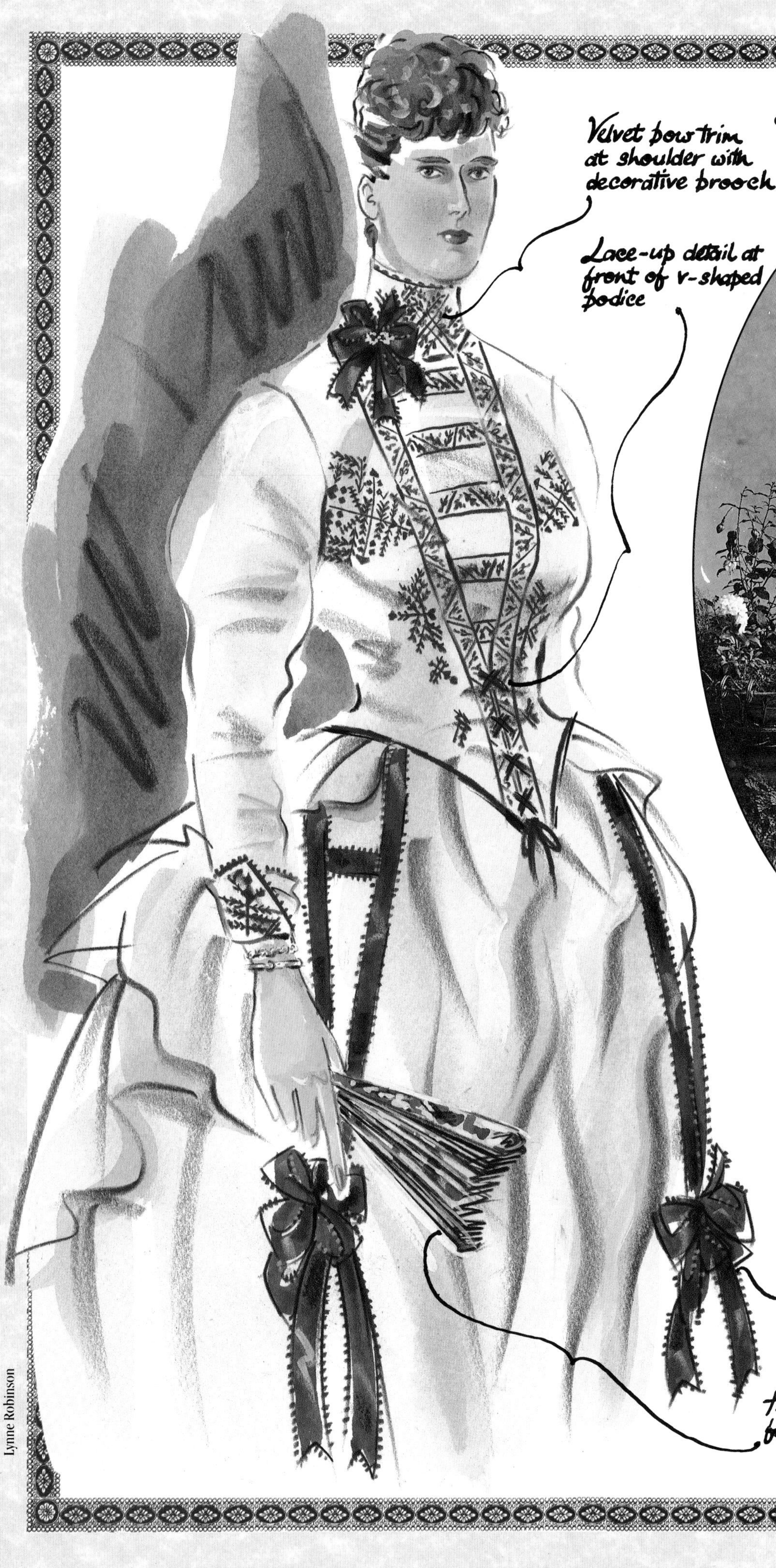

The muslin dress *left* was worn by Queen Mary when she was a young girl. The bodice, which is fitted to accentuate the waist, is embroidered with a leaf pattern that is continued elsewhere on the dress. A bustle fills out the back of the skirt while layers of muslin hang in loose folds at the front

Lynne Robinson

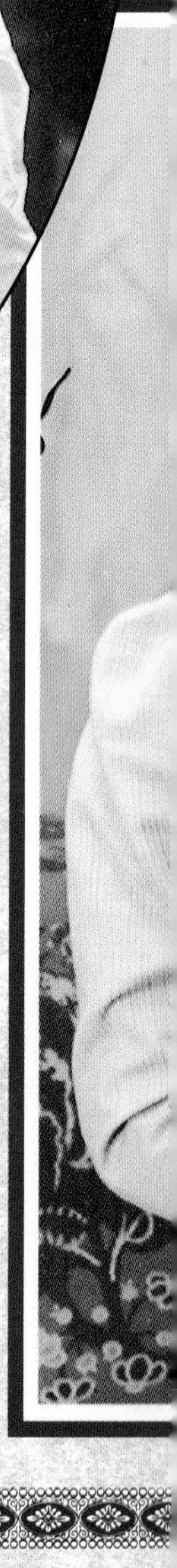

THE QUEEN MARY LOOK

As a girl, May's wardrobe followed the fashion trends of the day. But after her marriage to George, May's style was very much influenced by her husband. His desire that she look the same as she did when young led her to ignore the changes in fashion and adopt a stable and stylized form of dress that she was to retain for the rest of her life

👑 May's wedding gown *right* was made from white satin and covered with a silver design of interwoven roses, shamrocks, thistles and orange-flowers. Her décolletage is edged with lace and decorated with one of the lengths of flowers that are attached to the dress

👑 Worn while she was still the Duchess of York, this day dress *below* features a panel of spotted fabric set into the bodice, giving the illusion of a waistcoat closed by a long row of small buttons

Orange flowers, myrtle and white heather adorn the gown

Tiers of white lace cover the bust line and skirt of the wedding dress

Hulton Picture Company

Narrow brimmed straw hat with bound edge, trimmed with silk flowers and upright plume and draped with net

♛ Mary's blouse *left* is overlaid with tulle under a short-sleeved lace jacket. The embroidered collar echoes the design of the stomacher, and braid runs down the skirt to a repeated motif around the hem

High collar with silk ribbon and openwork embroidery

Panel of appliquéd and woven silk ribbons looped onto covered buttons on front of satin cummerbund

♛ *Above* Dressed for a fashionable wedding in a fringed dress and coat with appliqué velvet flowers. The coat, toque and parasol became Mary's hallmark

Lynne Robinson

Hulton Picture Company

♛ *Right* A formal late Victorian evening-gown of moiré taffeta and tulle, decorated with jet beads. Mary early developed a taste for jewels and stomachers to fill the bodice from neck to waist

11-stranded pearl choker with diamond studded spacers in the form of flowers

Diamond-studded stomacher

Hulton Picture Company

♛ **George** *above* **dressed with Edwardian elegance, but never knotted his tie, preferring to draw it through a ring instead**

THE SAILOR PRINCE AND CINDERELLA

JUST A FEW WEEKS AFTER THE UNUSED BRIDAL WREATH WAS LAID UPON THE COFFIN OF THE DUKE OF CLARENCE, THE SHY PRINCESS MARY WAS BETROTHED TO HIS BROTHER, AND A DEEP AND LASTING LOVE FLOWERED UNEXPECTEDLY BETWEEN THEM

W HO WAS TO MARRY THE FUTURE KING OF England? Prince Eddy's choice of bride was a major issue in the minds of the most important people in the land, from Queen Victoria down. 'A good sensible wife with some considerable character is what he needs most, but where is she to be found?' his father, the Prince of Wales, asked in despair.

One young Princess admirably fitted the description. May was already becoming known as a serious-minded young lady, sensible, reliable, dutiful and dedicated to good works. The fact of her morganatic descent, however, meant that no one would dare suggest her as a possible future Queen.

A Queen chooses a Queen

But only one person could make the suggestion without causing offence, and that one person was also a shrewd judge of character, dismissive of the more absurd aspects of protocol. Queen Victoria knew a good prospect when she saw one, and Princess May was her emphatic choice for Prince Eddy. She liked the modest, restrained way in which May conducted herself. She knew that her phlegmatic qualities would be excellent in a Queen Consort and that she would act as an essential stabilizing influence on Prince Albert Victor.

At the beginning of December 1891, Eddy did his duty and asked May to marry him. 'To my great surprise Eddy proposed to me,' May wrote in her diary. 'Of course I said yes – We are both very happy.' The wedding was to be in February, and Princess May went with her parents to stay with Eddy and his family so that they could all be together for his 28th birthday. But he became ill the day before and, just one week after his birthday, Eddy died of flu complicated by pneumonia. What sort of a king Eddy would have made is open to speculation, but it is probably fair to say that his family's loss

♛ Destined to be Queen: no one thought 'poor May' with her flawed ancestry would ever marry, but Cinderella had a fairy godmother. Her engagement to the Duke of Clarence below lasted only five weeks but, within 18 months, Victoria had arranged for her to marry the Duke of York right. Obediently he proposed and obediently she accepted – and, more spontaneously, they fell in love

♛ As Princess of Teck below right May occupied the position of poor relation; a target for contempt and condescension from her Royal relations. In choosing her as a successor, Victoria brought about a truly successful marriage – one in which May's unique qualities could be used to the full in guiding the monarchy through the shoals of the next century

Popperfoto

By gracious permission of
HM the Queen

She was not alone in thinking this a very good idea. Within weeks of Eddy's death, all the family had come round to the view that this would be the best outcome for all, and George was amenable to persuasion. But it is not the easiest matter in the world to woo the fiancée of your recently dead brother, especially if you are not much practised in the art of courtship.

The family did what they could by making sure the young couple were put in the way of each other as much as possible. Shortly after Prince Eddy's death, the Wales and Teck families were both recovering from the shock and the distress by spending some time on the French Riviera. Prince George and his parents were at Cap Martin, Princess May and her family were close by in Cannes.

The matchmaking must have seemed transparently obvious to the young pair but both tried their best to do what was expected of them. George laboured over his love notes: in one he finished lamely that he hoped 'this won't bore you too much, when you are, stop

was the country's gain. Now Georgie was the oldest surviving son of the Prince of Wales, in direct line to the throne.

A new heir

Prince George himself was very ill at this time and at one point it was feared that he too would die. He was 26 years old, grieving for his brother and still weak from his illness. His whole life had changed; no longer was he destined for a life at sea, but he would have to study to prepare himself for the throne.

In keeping with his new status, in the summer of 1892 Queen Victoria created Prince George the Duke of York. He was granted a suitable income, two houses and a household of servants. Now he too needed to be fitted up with the right wife for the job.

Queen Victoria had thought long and hard about May's suitability. Now that Eddy was dead Victoria was reluctant to relinquish her image of May as Queen, and she quickly proposed that the young woman transfer her hand and her affections to the new heir.

Hulton Picture Company

Topham

to behave with exemplary good manners and had no practice in coquettish behaviour.

'I am very sorry that I am still so shy with you,' she wrote to George after one of their meetings. 'I tried not to be so the other day, but alas failed, I was angry with myself. It is so stupid to be so stiff together and really there is nothing I would not tell you except that I love you more than anybody in the world, and this I cannot tell you myself so I write it to relieve my feelings.' Prince George felt his own deficiencies as a fiancé and would have liked to be different too. 'Thank God we both understand each other, and I think it really unnecessary for me to tell you how deep my love for you my darling is and I feel it growing stronger and stronger every time I see you, although I may appear shy and cold,' he wrote.

A great occasion

The wedding was to be on 6 July 1893 at the Chapel Royal, St James's Palace. The presents poured in: 1500 arrived in all, with a value of around £300,000 – the equivalent of several million pounds today.

'There is not even any pretence at love-making'

LADY IN WAITING ON MAY

Hulton Picture Company

♛ *Prince Eddy's death shocked the country, and his funeral above top was a day of national mourning. The saddest and most moving moment of the ceremony occurred when the Prince of Wales laid the wreath of orange blossoms – that May, the bereaved betrothed, above was to wear at her wedding – on her dead fiancé's coffin*

and throw it away'. To the delight of everyone the courtship had begun.

Extraordinary rumours

At the end of April 1893, while George was in Rome, his resolve was stiffened by the circulation of a rumour that he was already secretly married to an American woman. 'The story of my being already married to an American is really very amusing,' he wrote to his father's private secretary. By 3 May he was back in England and proposing to May in the garden of Sheen Lodge, Richmond. The same day the *Star* related the rumour to its readers. The Duke of York, it said, had lately contracted a secret marriage with the daughter of a British Naval officer. 'I say, May,' he told his fiancée jokingly, 'we can't get married after all. I hear I have got a wife and three children.'

The strange courtship was watched with concern by those who loved them, and glee by those who didn't. The lady-in-waiting to May's grandmother wrote waspishly in her diary, 'It is clear that there is not even any pretence at love-making. May is radiant in her position and abundantly satisfied, but placid and cold as always, the Duke of York apparently nonchalantly indifferent.' But underneath the surface things were beginning to change. May was starting to fall in love with her husband-to-be. She very much wanted to make him fall in love with her, but she had been brought up always

The big day dawned exceptionally hot. Queen Victoria was in high spirits. She wore her own wedding veil under a small coronet, and wedding lace over her black dress.

Victoria's verdict was that May looked 'very sweet'. She described the bride's outfit minutely. 'Her dress was very simple, of white satin with a silver design of roses, shamrocks, thistles and orange flowers, interwoven. On her head she had a small wreath of orange flowers, myrtle and white heather surmounted by the diamond necklace I gave her, which can also be worn as a diadem, and her mother's wedding veil.' The bridegroom wore the ceremonial uniform of a captain in the Royal Navy. He waited at the altar while May was brought down the aisle by her father and brother. The same lady-in-waiting who had commented so adversely on the courtship was unimpressed by the bride: 'Instead of coming in the exquisite, ideal way the Princess of Wales did at her wedding with her eyes cast down too prettily, May looked right and left and slightly bowed to her acquaintances! A great mistake.'

Queen Victoria had no such reservations. She thought it had all gone off perfectly. 'Georgie gave his answers very distinctly, while May, though quite self-possessed, spoke very low.'

May and George drove back to Buckingham Palace in the midst of cheering crowds, who were enjoying the fine weather nearly as much as the royal occasion. 'The heat was very

Hulton Picture Company

great, quite overwhelming,' Queen Victoria wrote. 'Very soon the Bride and Bridegroom arrived, and I stepped out on the balcony with them, taking her by the hand, which produced another great outburst of cheering.' The honeymoon was spent at the newly renamed York Cottage, in the grounds of Sandringham House, which was to be their home for the next 33 years. Previously the cottage had been called Bachelors' Cottage, a more appropriate name given its size. But when Bertie decided to give it to the newlyweds as a wedding present, he also had it redecorated and enlarged.

Settling into the new home

The improvements were only just finished in time for the honeymoon, and the place still smelled of fresh paint when they arrived. The house had been furnished from top to bottom with brand-new furniture, which George had chosen on his own to surprise his bride. Even the wallpaper and carpets were new.

May was understandably disappointed to be presented with this *fait accompli*. She was too modest and polite to complain, but George could not but be aware that she was upset. He was truly astonished — his father had prepared the family home in exactly the same way for *his* bride.

☞ **Below** *Cannes, where the grief-stricken George sought comfort from his 'dear Miss May' and found that he had fallen in love with the quiet little cousin* **inset** *who would become the mainstay of his life. George* **left** *spent every possible moment of his carefully arranged five-day visit with May, and Queen Victoria was delighted, though a full year of mourning had to elapse before the proposal*

Hulton Picture Company

'*I love you more than anybody in the world, and this I cannot tell you myself so I write it*'

MARY

♔ *The awkwardness of the stage-managed courtship had been defeated by the power of the shy young couple's love, and the wedding itself was 'the greatest success ever seen or heard of'. The official photograph* right *was taken after the ceremony in the Chapel Royal* below *where an error in protocol had resulted in Victoria's arriving first instead of last. She insisted on entering straight away and said it was 'very amusing to see everyone come in'*

THE TROUSSEAU

The wedding dress with may flowers and the extravagant trousseau ordered by Bertie and Alix during May's engagement to Eddy was packed away and eventually lost. Fortunately, a present from 'Aunt Augusta' – the Grand Duchess of Mecklenburg-Strelitz – enabled Mary and her mother to order a replacement trousseau of 40 outdoor suits, 15 ball dresses and five tea-gowns as well as matinée gowns, travelling capes, travelling wraps, driving capes and of course quantities of bonnets, shoes and gloves. The *Lady's Pictorial* described in minute detail every dress, made exclusively by English dressmakers. Princess Mary Adelaide told the press: 'I am determined that all the silk shall come from England, all the flannel from Wales, all the tweeds from Scotland and every yard of lace and poplin from Ireland'

What May could do was arrange the furniture as she liked. She spent much of the first week of marriage reorganizing rooms and changing pictures around. She was delighted with the possibilities of her new home. 'The cottage is very nice but very small. However, I think we can make it charming,' she wrote. Archbishop Lang visited, and was shown all over the house by the young couple. He was touched by their enthusiasm – 'a quite charming and almost naive keenness. It might have been a curate and his wife in their new house.' It was to be a quiet honeymoon. The newlyweds needed the time to get to know each other better and to learn to be easy with each other. But after just two weeks their isolation was disrupted.

Alix, missing her darling son, swooped down on them with a party of eight others and a pack of dogs. She didn't think much of May's tentative home-making and thought she could do much better herself. While May was out one day she organized the servants to rearrange the furniture and pictures as she thought fit.

George was caught between his adored Motherdear and new wife. 'We can move it all back again in a minute . . .' he wrote to May. But, fearing her mother-in-law and still insecure as a wife, May decided to leave it as it was.

The spiteful sisters

The truth was that Alexandra was jealous of May's position in her son's life. She took to dropping in at all times, even during breakfast, and bringing George's sisters with her. They, too, had little liking for May. They knew she was better educated than they were and mistook her shyness for arrogance. George's sister

Victoria once said to a fellow guest, 'Now do try to talk to May at dinner, though one knows she is deadly dull.' Louise patronized her behind her back: 'Poor May! Poor May! With her Württemberg hands!' To May, this invasion of her marital home by her husband's boisterous, critical relatives was an ordeal. It was hard enough for her to adjust to married life without this. 'I sometimes think that just after we were married we were not left alone enough and had not the opportunity of learning to understand each other as quickly as we might otherwise have done, and this led to many little rubs which might have been avoided,' she wrote to him some time later. 'You see we are both terribly sensitive and the slightest sharp word said by one to the other immediately gave offence and I fear that neither you nor I forget those things in a hurry.'

But, despite everything, the miracle had occurred. The arranged marriage had turned into a love-match. They were ideally suited and, within a year of marriage, were deeply in love. They always found it difficult to share their most tender feelings with each other except on paper, which May occasionally lamented. But it means that we have a touching record of their developing love. 'When I asked you to marry me, I was very fond of you, but not very much in love with you,' George wrote in the months after their wedding. 'I have tried to understand you and to know you and with the happy result that I know now that I do *love* you darling girl with all my *heart*, and am simply *devoted* to you . . . *I adore you sweet May.* I can't say more than that.'

♛ *Queen Victoria was not the only one to think York Cottage below an inauspicious place to begin married life. May's new home was practically in her mother-in-law's garden and everything she did was reported to, discussed with, and usually criticized by, the Princess of Wales, who could not forget that May should have married Eddy*

Hulton Picture Company

PROUD HERITAGE

The Edwardian age formally ended on 22 June 1911 when King George V and Queen Mary were crowned at Westminster and the monarchy entered upon a new chapter in its history. The Great War changed the world, the Royal Family changed its name and three mighty Emperors fell, but George and Mary stood as rocks in the swirling tides of the 20th century, majestic symbols of Britain's great Royal tradition. Both the King and Queen considered the throne as a sacred trust and the regalia associated with the monarchy as the outward symbol of its honour, embodying a thousand years of British glory

By gracious permission of HM the Queen

John Frost

HONI SOIT QUI MAL Y PENSE

DIEU ET MON DROIT

Left The Royal Arms of Great Britain in the form used in England, Wales and Northern Ireland. The Scottish unicorn is uncrowned and supports the sinister (left) side of the shield. The crest is the English Royal crest and the shield is surrounded by the device of the Order of the Garter. *Dieu et mon droit* is the English Royal motto

Below Knights of the Order of the Bath, which was founded in 1399. Its name derives from the night before King Henry IV's Coronation, when the friends who were to form his escort at the ceremony took a ritual bath at the Chapel of St John at the Tower of London. The King marked a cross in water on their backs and later formed the Order

Their Majesties at the Beginning of the Reign.

John Frost

Above The Coronation robes. The Sovereign wears the Imperial State Crown on leaving the Abbey. Queen Mary's crown was designed for the occasion, incorporating the Koh-i-noor diamond at the front

Both pictures (details) by Richard Jack 1926/27 by gracious permission of HM the Queen

♛ *Above* King George is wearing the Robes of the Order of the Garter. The oldest Order of Christian chivalry, it was established by Edward III on St George's Day, 1348. The name is said to derive from an incident at a ball: King Edward was dancing with his cousin, Joan, Countess of Salisbury. Her blue garter fell to the floor and the King picked it up, saying to the laughing courtiers *Honi soit qui mal y pense* (Evil be to him who evil thinks). These words have since become the Order's motto.

The diamond-set Garter Star is pinned on George's chest, while another Star is embroidered on his dark-blue velvet Robes. The Garter Collar, 24 gold plaques showing the Garter surrounding a red Tudor rose, is worn over his shoulders; hanging from it is the Great George, a heavy, bejewelled badge in the form of St George slaying the dragon

♛ *Left* Queen Mary wears the cornflower-blue Riband of the Order, the diamond Star and, on her right hip, the Lesser George badge with its cameo of St George set in diamonds and rubies. The diamond-encrusted garter embroidered with the motto is worn on her left arm, and her Robes are on the balustrade behind her. On her head is the tiara of 15 interlaced diamond circles hung with Oriental pearls made for Grand Duchess Vladimir around 1890 and smuggled out of Russia during the revolution. Mary bought the tiara in 1921

👑 *Right* The orders, medals and badges created by King George V: **1** *Distinguished Flying Cross*, **2** *Distinguished Flying Medal*, **3** *Air Force Medal*, **4** *Air Force Cross*, **5** *British War Medal*, **6** *1914 Star*, **7** *1915 Star*, **8** *Victory Medal*, **9** *Military Cross*, **10** *Companion of Honour*, **11** *Badge, Order of the British Empire*, **12** *Baronet's Badge*, **13** *Distinguished Service Medal*, **14** *Military Medal*, **15** *Knight Bachelor's Badge*, **16** *Special Constabulary Medal*, **17** *Territorial War Medal*, **18** *Mercantile Marine Medal*, **19** *New General Service Medal*, **20** *Naval General Service Medal*

👑 The Imperial Crown of India *below* was made especially for King George to wear at the Delhi Durbar in 1911, as the Imperial State Crown must not leave Britain. The crown – which cost £60,000 and was paid for by the Indian Government – contains 6170 diamonds, plus numerous emeralds, sapphires and rubies

Queen Mary's Crown *below right* was made for the Coronation. It originally held the Third and Fourth Stars of Africa, which were cut from the huge Cullinan diamond (a gift to Edward from the Government of the Transvaal). They are mounted in such a way that they can easily be removed and worn as a brooch. They now belong to Queen Elizabeth

IN THE SHADOW OF THE THRONE

THE DEATH OF QUEEN VICTORIA SIGNALLED THE END OF BLISSFUL OBSCURITY FOR THE YORKS AS THEY MOVED A STEP NEARER THE THRONE TO BECOME PRINCE AND PRINCESS OF WALES

Hulton Picture Company

A S WELL AS YORK COTTAGE THE YOUNG couple had a London residence, York House, a corner of St James's Palace. This was on a much grander scale than the Norfolk residence, and for this reason George, in particular, preferred the country house. He hated entertaining, and at York Cottage he had the excuse that the rooms were too small for anything formal.

It was almost too small for anything at all, as far as May was concerned. She hoped to have children soon and there was nowhere to put them. So she sought permission from Alix to extend the house. She added a three-storey wing in roughcast and pebble-dash, with black mock Tudor beams and a wooden-railed balcony. She linked this addition to the main cottage by a small tower with slate turret.

Royal duties

The Yorks were allowed to get away with very few Royal duties or formal entertaining. Although in direct line of succession they seemed to most people very remote from the throne. George's parents, the Prince and Princess of Wales, did most of the deputizing for Queen Victoria, and loved it. George, anyway, was only just learning what it would mean to be king. At 28 he had been assigned a tutor to brush up on constitutional history.

Both George and May were relieved that they were not called upon to 'be royal' more often. Both were awkward in public and had little small-talk, but it sometimes had to be done.

Their first dinner party was held on 4 March 1894 at York House. They invited members of the family and laid on a lavish feast. This was a practice run for their first formal dinner party a few days later, given in honour of the new Prime Minister, Lord Rosebery.

These were an ordeal for May, who was five months pregnant. 'She is pretty and what you

would call voluptuous,' Sir Henry Ponsonby told his wife after sitting next to May at dinner, 'but decidedly dull.'

May was becoming increasingly shy and reserved. In the shadow of her glamorous mother-in-law with whom it would be impossible to compete, she fell back on glacial good manners.

The Queen was one of the few people to see beyond May's abrupt, stiff manner to the woman beneath. 'Each time I see you I love and respect you more,' Victoria wrote, 'and am so truly thankful that Georgie has such a partner.'

And of course Georgie was growing to love and need May more as the months went by. Away with his father at a State funeral, he wrote to her, 'I really believe I should get ill if I had to be away from you for a long time.'

A secure love

May was now quite secure in his love. 'Georgie is a dear,' she wrote to her old governess. 'He adores me which is touching. He likes reading to people so I jumped at this and he is going to read me some of his favourite books ... I am very glad I am married and don't feel at all strange, in fact I feel as if I had been married for years and quite settled down.'

Their first child was born on 23 June 1894 at White Lodge, Richmond Park. Queen Victoria ('What joy! What blessing!') wanted this future successor to the throne to be called Albert. But George and May had already decided that their first son's first name would be

👑 *This 'four generations' photograph* above *portrays Queen Victoria, Bertie, George and the newest heir to the throne, David. Victoria was very pleased with George and Mary's children – they were strong and healthy, good-natured and well-mannered. Bertie was also extremely fond of his grandchildren and, unlike Victoria, did not intimidate them*

👑 *George and May as they were in the early years of their marriage* left. *With the pressure of the throne still far removed from their lives, these were the happiest of times for the couple*

👑 *Although York Cottage had, at first, been an unpleasant place to begin her life with George, Mary was soon able to redecorate the little house to suit her own tastes. Right A view of Mary's cosy sitting-room where she spent many hours quietly reading and sewing*

Hulton Picture Company

The birth of George and May's first son was a happy occasion; above Mary and her mother admire David. But as their family continued to increase in number below it was clear that Mary was not instinctively maternal. Most of the actual 'mothering' was done by nannies. And while Mary loved her children and would put aside a little time each day to read or explain things to them, she was seldom affectionate and never played with them. However, young George right and the rest of the children retained many pleasant memories of the times they did spend with their parents, and they were, of course, spoiled by their adoring grandparents

Edward, after Prince Eddy, and he was known in the family by his last name, David.

The start of their family cemented their relationship – in their case this old cliché happened to be true. George was not inclined to be a womanizer, unlike his father, and he delighted in spending time with his wife and children.

All the rest of the children were born in York Cottage. The second son, Bertie, was born on 14 December 1895, the anniversary of Prince Albert's death. Princess Mary was born in 1897, Prince Henry in 1900, Prince George in 1902 and Prince John in 1905. George adored his children when they were babies, and his idea of a good evening was giving one of the young ones a bath and then settling by the fireside with his wife to read aloud to her.

Victoria's great-grandchildren

Queen Victoria was very approving of May and George's steady marriage, so different from the ups and downs and infidelities that marked the marriage of Bertie and Alix. Victoria was also much more taken with their children who were, in the main, sturdy and healthy like both their parents and, although high-spirited, much better behaved.

Bertie adored his grandchildren too, and dropped into York Cottage whenever he was passing – alone or with friends. He even gave up his pet bears who romped dangerously in the bearpit near York Cottage. In the interests of his grandchildren's safety he had the pit filled in and donated the bears to London Zoo.

The early years of married life passed happily and uneventfully. George was allowed to pursue the life of a country squire. He loved shooting, and became the best shot in the Royal Family. Much of the rest of the time was spent

Hulton Picture Company

quietly with his wife and children or going over his stamp collection.

It is often said that George and May were not good parents, that they treated their children coldly and unkindly. But when their children were small they seemed as happy as most children of their class and generation. As a guest once noted, 'The two little princes are splendid little boys and chattered away the whole of their lunch time, not the faintest shyness.' They were allowed a considerable amount of freedom to roam the estates on their bicycles or run around on the Sandringham golf course, and were utterly spoiled with presents on birthdays and Christmas. George taught the boys how to shoot and 'those small days,' wrote the Duke of Windsor later, 'provided some of my happiest memories of him'.

Royal pranks

Although George was a man with a high temper, he was fond of a joke. The older Princes used to play practical jokes on him, and he roared with laughter as the joke-shop spoon melted in his tea.

May's best friend Mabell, the Countess of Airlie, was distressed by the rumours about May and George. It was unfair that they were 'depicted as stern unloving parents . . . this they most certainly were not. Remembering them

Hulton Picture Company

RUMOURS

Gossip that George was already married did not go away after his wedding. The rumours continued to dog him right through until he became King. That year a republican newspaper, *The Liberator*, published an article titled 'Sanctified Bigamy', which said that in 1890 George had married the daughter of Admiral Sir Michael Culme-Seymour while in Malta and had children by her. When his brother had died, the article asserted, George had 'foully abandoned his true wife and entered a sham and shameful marriage with a daughter of the Duke of Teck'.

The author was sued for criminal libel and the trial proved, among other things, that he had not been in Malta during the time stated and that the island's registers showed no record of the alleged marriage. The author was sentenced to a year in jail

John Frost

♛ George and May sit uncomfortably in the spacious surroundings of their apartments in St James's Palace below. The couple's preference for their beloved York Cottage and their unease in royal social situations hinted at the fact that they were somewhat ill-prepared for the grandeur and responsibilities that would accompany their future roles as Prince and Princess of Wales and, later, King and Queen

in early years at Sandringham before their family was complete, I believe they were conscientious and more truly devoted to their children than the majority of parents of that era. The tragedy was that neither had any understanding of a child's mind.'

The children were treated like little adults, and were supposed to bear their lot with fortitude. George saw it as character-forming for his children to fear him. 'My father was frightened of his mother; I was frightened of my father,' he is said to have remarked, 'and I am damned well going to see to it that my children are frightened of me.' He teased them constantly, enjoying little Mary's fiery blush and unaware that little Bertie's stammer might be his fault.

'While affection was certainly not lacking in my upbringing,' the Duke of Windsor later wrote, 'the mere circumstances of my father's

'I thank God every day that I have such a wife as you'

GEORGE

position interposed an impalpable barrier that inhibited the closer continuing intimacy of conventional family life.'

May was gentler with the children. She did not enjoy the business of giving birth and was not terribly interested in babies. It was the custom for upper-class children to be almost exclusively looked after by nurses in the first years of their lives, and this suited May well.

But May loved spending time with her children when they grew older and became more interesting. They were among the very few

Hulton Picture Company

people who knew that she had a sense of humour, and her sitting-room was a refuge for the children. Indeed they spent so much time with their mother quietly sewing that all the boys became expert at needle-point.

May protected them as well as she could from their father's rages, but her first loyalty was to him. Her strict sense of hierarchy meant that she thought her husband was the most important person in the household.

The quiet life of the Yorks changed after 22 January 1901, when Queen Victoria died. Now Bertie was on the throne, becoming the almost unrecognizably dignified King Edward VII, and George was the heir apparent.

Life in the public eye

The couple were now expected to fulfil their fair share of Royal duties, and in March 1901 the Duke and Duchess of York embarked on a tour of Australia.

George, as usual, kept a methodical diary of the happenings. He was never very good at descriptive passages, but excellent on statistics. They were away from the family for 231 days, during which time they covered 45,000 miles, laid 21 foundation stones, received 544 addresses, presented 4329 medals, reviewed 62,000 troops and shook hands with 24,000 people at official receptions.

Soon after their return he wrote to May: 'Somehow I can't tell you, so I take the opportunity of writing to say how deeply I am indebted to you darling for the splendid way in which you supported and helped me during our long tour. It was you who made it a success.' He continued, 'Although I have often told you before, I repeat it once more, that I love you darling child, with my whole heart and soul, and I thank God every day that I have such a wife as you, who is such a great help and support to me and I believe loves me too.'

Prince and Princess of Wales

On their return the King created George and May Prince and Princess of Wales. They were titles that sat rather uneasily on the new holders: Bertie and Alix had held the titles for so long that they were firmly associated with the older couple in people's minds.

The new King also thought it was fitting for his heir to move into more spacious premises. But although George agreed to move into Marlborough House on his parents' removal to Buckingham Palace, nothing would persuade him to give up York Cottage.

In 1905 the Prince and Princess of Wales went on their first tour of India. They enjoyed themselves enormously and George began to show his qualities as a statesman in training. He made notes for his father on everything he saw

By gracious permission of HM the Queen

👑 **Above 'Fancy you "Miss May" on an Elephant!'** *was Alexandra's response to her daughter-in-law's letter from India. George and Mary's trip was a great success, and left them with many fond memories*

👑 **The magnificent Coronation ceremony** *below was attended by 7000 people, including an impressive array of distinguished guests, all of whom crowded into the Abbey to watch George and Mary's majestic transformation*

and put forward a strong case for home rule by the Indians. It was one of the very few trips abroad that George enjoyed, and he was sorry when it ended. May remembered their last view of India from the deck of the ship with romantic nostalgia. 'We went on the bridge and watched dear beautiful India vanish from our sight.'

Bertie was determined to train his son for the throne. Queen Victoria had never allowed him to see a state paper, but he involved George from the start. He expected George to read the Cabinet and Foreign Office papers,

THE ROYAL STAMP OF APPROVAL

One of the greatest loves of George's life was his stamp collection. He set out to make it the most comprehensive collection of British and Commonwealth stamps in the world and often asked friends and colonial Governors and High Commissioners to find stamps for him.

He also bought specimens to fill gaps, writing the price he paid under each one in the album. 'Did your Royal Highness hear that some damned fool has just paid £1450 for a single stamp?' a courtier once asked him. 'I was the damned fool,' he replied.

By the time of his death the investments looked less foolish. His collection consisted of 250,000 stamps in 325 large volumes, and is reckoned to be priceless.

Among the rarer specimens in his collection is the Tyrian Plum *right*, which was used to send a letter to George on the day he became King. On account of the late King's death, this stamp, which bears an image of his head, was withdrawn before it could be issued officially

By gracious permission of HM the Queen

The Royal couple pose in the Robing room of the House of Lords right for an official portrait to mark the opening of Parliament in 1911. Taken after the accession and before the Coronation, this was the first official photograph of George and Mary in their new roles as King and Queen. Mary, resplendent in diamonds, wears a black beaded gown in mourning for King Edward

Hutton Picture Company

attend debates in the House of Lords and dine with leading statesmen of the day.

With these duties, which George found onerous, came the onset of ill-health. He started to suffer from chronic dyspepsia, which was almost certainly due to nerves. The idea of becoming King worried him enormously. He admired his father and did not know how he would manage when he finally took his place.

Succeeding to the throne

But the day came less than ten years after Bertie had succeeded. On 6 May 1910 Edward VII died and George became King. 'I have lost my best friend and the best of fathers,' he wrote in his diary on the night of his father's death. 'But God will help me in my great responsibilities and darling May will be my comfort as she has always been. May God give me strength and guidance in the heavy task which has fallen upon me.'

On 22 June 1911, the Abbey was filled with people awaiting the arrival of George and Mary for the start of the Coronation ceremony. An audible murmur arose when they finally entered. The Queen wore a brilliant tiara (later replaced by the Coronation Crown with the Koh-i-noor diamond) and deep purple velvet robes lined with ermine over her embroidered white satin gown. The King appeared in his crimson Robe of State with an ermine cape and the Cap of Maintenance on his head.

After the three-hour ceremony, George and Mary returned to Buckingham Palace for a heavily scheduled day. George's diary concludes, 'Rather tired. Bed at 11.45. Beautiful illuminations everywhere.'

By gracious permission of HM the Queen

ROYAL RESIDENCE

SANDRINGHAM HOUSE

Edward VII bought the Sandringham Estate in Norfolk from Charles Spencer Cowper, nephew of Lord Palmerston, for £220,000 in 1861. The original low, white house was largely replaced by the present red brick mansion in 1870. 'Dear old Sandringham, the place I love better than anywhere else in the world,' wrote George V, who had known it since he was a small boy. It was here, in 1932, that he made his first Christmas radio broadcast

♔ Sandringham House was designed by Albert Humbert in the style of a Jacobean country house, according to the instructions of his client, Edward VII, who insisted that traditional gables and chimneys should be retained. A ballroom, library and other features were added one by one, giving the house its rambling character

⚜ **The Main Drawing Room** *left*, which leads into the Dining Room, is where the Royal Family and their guests gather before dinner. Queen Victoria was very impressed by this room when she first visited the new house, describing it in her diary as a 'very long and handsome drawing room with painted ceiling and panels with two fireplaces'. The portrait of Princess Victoria is one of three by Edward Hughes who also painted Alexandra and Maud in 1896. Decorating the screen are photographs of politicians and other eminent people of the day

⚜ **The Ballroom** *right*. The walls are hung with an impressive collection of Indian weapons, presented to Edward during his state visit in 1875–76. The fireplace is designed along classical lines, set in a shallow alcove with flanking Corinthian pillars. The pediment over the mirror echoes the magnificent mouldings above the doors, while benches along the panelled walls provide seating for weary dancers

⚜ **This veneered writing desk** *left* stands in the Main Drawing Room and bears twin photographs of George and Mary. It was made for Sandringham in 1863 by Holland & Sons and cost £31.17s.0d

♛ The walls of the Main Dining Room *above* feature decorative tapestry panels. The designs are woven after cartoons by seven Spanish artists including Goya

By gracious permission of HM the Queen

By gracious permission of HM the Queen

♔ The Small Drawing Room *left* is used by the lady-in-waiting in attendance on the Queen. The recessed display case on the left of the fireplace contains a priceless collection of fine European porcelain. Among the pictures are portraits of Alexandra's parents and of two of her daughters, Louise and Victoria

♔ The Saloon *left* is the largest room in the house, being two storeys high. It serves as both entrance hall and main reception room – the Royal Family and their guests spend the evening here after dinner, as well as using it as a convenient assembly point. The main feature of the room is the imposing Minstrel's Gallery. The walls of the Saloon are decorated with three large 17th-century Brussels tapestries illustrating the history of the Roman Emperor Constantine, and next to the fireplace hangs a painting of Bertie, Alix and two of their children, Eddy and Maud

♔ The house is filled with display cases housing all kinds of remarkable collections, reflecting Mary's favourite hobby. This cabinet *right* stands in the Main Drawing Room and contains 18th-century Worcester porcelain. The oval tea caddy and cover in the Japanese style (on the second lowest shelf) is a particularly notable piece

Hulton Picture Company

👑 *Above* The King shooting at Balmoral. While some did not approve of George's hobby, he delighted in the sport all through his life and found it very relaxing

👑 Lavery's charming conversation piece of the King and Queen with their eldest son, David, and their daughter, Mary *right* was one of the few Royal commissions that pleased George. Other artists – such as Charles Sim – were not so fortunate. Sim's attempt to portray the King in an elegant pose resulted in George's claim that he had been made to look like a ballet dancer and he ordered the painting destroyed

👑 *Far right* The King and Queen open the new galleries at the Tate. George was notorious for his scepticism about 'modern' art and his visits to exhibitions were always memorable occasions. This one was no exception. As he stood before a work of a French Impressionist, he called out, 'Here's something to make you laugh, May'

By gracious permission of HM the Queen

DUTY AND DEVOTION

ON 6 MAY 1920 GEORGE V ENTERED UPON HIS HERITAGE. THE NEW KING AND EMPEROR WROTE IN HIS DIARY, 'MAY GOD GIVE ME STRENGTH AND GUIDANCE IN THE HEAVY TASK WHICH HAS FALLEN UPON ME'

THIS NEW KING AND QUEEN WERE VERY different from the last. Physically Edward VII and Alexandra had been magnificent, but there was something far more ordinary about George V and Queen Mary, as May was now known. He was not very tall – 5′ 6″ at most. May was the same height, but with her high heels, toque hats and erect posture she seemed to tower over her more sparely built husband with his slight stoop.

A quieter court

It soon became clear that their court was to be very different too. May's shyness now began to assume a more regal aura. Rather than mocking her for it, people began to stand in awe of her. The Edwardians had been sophisticated, amoral and fun. George and May had always disapproved of the older generation. 'Je n'aime pas leurs "goings on",' May had once said. Their own private life was lived with utmost respectability, and they wanted to see that reflected in the people they gathered around them. May

dreaded the prospect of court life. 'I regret the quieter, easier time we had, everything will be more difficult now and more ceremonious.'

One guest at Balmoral who had known both reigns described the new regime. 'It is altogether different here from former years,' he wrote. '… Yet everything is very charming and wholesome and sweet. The house is a home for children – six of them at luncheon – the youngest running around the table all the while. The Queen knits of an evening. Not a sign of "bridge". The King sat on the sofa talking with me until bedtime … Last night the French governess sat on the King's right hand at dinner. Imagine the courtiers of Berlin or Vienna if they could have seen!'

Conservative clothes

They were conservative in dress as well as morals. George wore the clothes of his youth throughout his life and, like his father, was a stickler for the right garment at the right time. He wore his trousers with the creases down the

By gracious permission of HM the Queen

THE DELHI DURBAR

George and Mary travelled to India to receive homage at a ceremony called the Durbar, held on 12 December 1911.

With her coronation robes the Queen wore the famous tiara of 15 interlocking circles and the Cambridge emeralds. The badge of the Star of India hung from a ribbon across her bodice. George wore the specially made Indian crown, a gift from the people of India. Both were seated on solid silver thrones encased in gold to receive homage from the Governor General and all the Indian ruling chiefs.

The Royal couple then walked in procession, holding hands, their trains carried by young princes. George announced that the capital would be transferred from Calcutta to Delhi, the ancient Mogul capital, and that a Governorship would be created for Bengal. The National Anthem was sung and 'the most wonderful Durbar ever held, was closed'

he took a turn around the garden. After lunch he slept in an armchair for exactly 15 minutes.

In the afternoon the King either attended an official engagement, played a game of tennis or spent a precious hour with his stamp collection. The early evening was devoted to matters of State and the day's dispatch boxes. Later he liked to dine quietly with his family, wearing white tie and the Order of the Garter. At any suggestion of an altered routine he would say, 'Well, we never did *that* in the olden days.'

George and May would sometimes dine out at the house of one of their friends or go to a popular play. When they stayed in he would read a biography, or they would listen to Gilbert and Sullivan or order a comedy or adventure film to be shown at the Palace cinema. At precisely 11.10 George would make his way to bed, pausing only to check the barometer before he retired.

'I knew no one who liked his comforts more,' said David of his father. 'Everything about him was always of the best – his clothes, his fine hammer guns by Purdey, his food, his stationery, his cigarette cases by Fabergé.'

Strict protocol

Formal entertaining at Windsor was as precisely organized as everything else in George V's life. For Ascot week, ladies were expected to bring two new dresses for the mornings, four outdoor outfits and five evening dresses to be worn with long white gloves that reached to their armpits.

side, and pulled his ties through a ring instead of knotting them. Queen Mary, who would have liked a bit of variety in her dress, only wore the colours and styles of which he approved, which meant that she was stuck in a time-warp too. She only defied him by wearing long earrings which, he complained, distorted her ears. She once longed to follow the fashion for slightly shorter skirts, because her legs were her best feature. Her friend, Lady Airlie, wore a skirt at the new length to test out George's reaction. May tentatively asked him whether he liked it. 'No, I didn't,' he said emphatically. 'It was too short.' So she wistfully abandoned the idea.

Settling into the Palace

Life soon assumed a steady routine. In a habit that remained from his sea-faring days, George started his day by consulting the barometer. He began work on his boxes at seven in the morning, wrote up his diary and read *The Times*.

Breakfast was served promptly at nine o'clock, after which he gave the rest of the morning to official business. Before lunch at precisely 1.30, at which he was joined by Mary,

Hulton Picture Company

♛ **Right** *The King talks to a little local boy during a visit to Sunderland in 1918. This was one of the most famous photographs of George ever taken, and shows the monarch in a confident mood*

♛ **Queen Mary and her only daughter at Buckingham Palace far right.** *The Princess Royal was a nurse during World War 1 and wears the VAD uniform*

♛ **Confused pre-schoolers at the Rachel McMillan College in Deptford are treated to a visit by the Queen below.** *Mary took a special interest in any organization devoted to the care of children*

♛ **Upset that he was unable to take a more active role during the war, George tried to compensate by making hundreds of visits to troops, hospitals, munition factories and shipyards. Included in these was his visit to Ypres** *below left where his own regiment, the Grenadier Guards, was stationed*

Popperfoto

COURT LIFE

Before dinner the men and women were separately lined up in order of precedence to shake hands with the King and Queen. The simple meal was accompanied by some chamber music, after which the ladies left and the King stayed to smoke a cigar and swap jokes with the men. He never lingered long; he wanted to be with his wife.

Understandably the fashionable set found court life very boring, and they were soon dropped from the visiting list, especially flirtatious ladies. 'We've seen enough of the intrigue and meddling of certain ladies,' he told a confidante. 'I'm not interested in any wife except my own.'

George found the business of being King hard. 'The most terrible ordeal I have ever gone through,' was how he described the events of 6 February 1911. He was referring to the State opening of Parliament, an annual duty he always loathed. But this did not mean that he skimped it. He chose to wear the Imperial State Crown despite the fact that the tradition of wearing it had ceased because it was so heavy (three and a half pounds). He wrote proudly in his diary: 'I wore my crown as many people wished it and it had not been worn for opening

Popperfoto

Popperfoto

John Frost

'We sailors never smile on duty'

GEORGE

♔ *The King stands at the helm of his yacht, the* Britannia *left. George loved to race and his yacht filled him with pride: 'As long as I live, I will never own any other yacht than* Britannia.*' When he died in 1936, the yacht was taken to deep waters south of the Isle of Wight and sunk*

♔ *The King convalesces at Bognor below in the spring of 1929 after surviving a near-fatal infection of the blood*

of Parliament for over 60 years.'

During the first few years of George's reign he did not make much impact on his people. He was a stickler for the ceremonial aspects of his role and the trappings of monarchy: crowns and sceptres, robes and regalia, but he was not yet seen as a warm man. 'We sailors never smile on duty,' he said. Queen Mary was also rarely seen to smile, but for a different reason. She confided to a friend that she avoided having photographs taken of herself smiling because, when she did, she 'looked like a horse'.

The Great War

The change in his people's perception of George came during the 1914–1918 War. War is a time when a country traditionally focuses attention on the sovereign, and George as figurehead was much appreciated. He was the most English of monarchs and, when it was suggested that he must be pro-German because the Royal Family had a German name, he 'started and grew pale', and shortly afterwards decreed that they should henceforward be known as the House of Windsor.

He resented what he saw as his almost useless role during the war. He wanted to go into battle with his regiment, the Grenadier Guards, but the Government wouldn't allow it. 'I feel such a swine having a soft comfortable time out here,' he wrote, 'while the Guards Division is at Ypres.' In 1915, while inspecting the troops in France, he injured himself badly by falling from his horse. He was 50 by then, and the injury caused him stiffness and pain the rest of his life.

The first great tragedy in May's life was the death of her youngest son, Prince John, at the age of 14 in 1919. He had been sickly all his life, and suffered from epilepsy. It was after one such attack that he died.

May's opponent

In addition to this tragedy, May had another thorn in her side: George's sister, Princess Victoria, continued to dislike May. She never married and had plenty of leisure to make May's life difficult. She spoke to George on the telephone every morning and often used the opportunity to say things against his wife. It caused Queen Mary to forever loathe the telephone.

York Cottage was still the favourite retreat of the Royal Family. Queen Alexandra continued to live on in solitary splendour in the 'Big House' at Sandringham, and many thought that it was 'Motherdear's' legendary selfishness that stopped her moving out to let the new

Hulton Picture Company

Seated before the microphone at a table covered with a heavy cloth to muffle the sound of rustling papers, the King delivers his Christmas message at Sandringham left. Although reluctant, he was finally persuaded to address the Empire for the first time in 1932

George and May were delighted when their second son married Lady Elizabeth Bowes Lyon in 1923, and they both adored their grandchildren, the little Princesses Elizabeth and Margaret, who often came to stay.

The children marry

The Royal couple were quite delighted as, one by one, their other children settled down. Prince George married the beautiful Princess Marina of Greece, then Princess Mary married Lord Harewood, and Prince Henry married Lady Alice Montagu-Douglas-Scott.

QUEEN MARY'S DOLLS' HOUSE

This extraordinary creation is the most magnificent dolls' house in the world. It took three years to complete the miniature grand house, which was designed by Sir Edwin Lutyens. It was built to the scale of one inch to the foot – Swift's description of the scale of Lilliput in *Gulliver's Travels*. Its gardens were tended by Miss Gertrude Jekyll, and Princess Marie Louise was put in charge of the library. Leading artists of the day decorated the walls and ceilings and painted tiny pictures to be hung in the rooms. There was a replica set of crown jewels in the strong room, toys in the nursery, gold frying-pans in the kitchen, a well-stocked larder and real wine in the bottles in the cellar. Contemporary authors donated miniatures of their books to the library and every detail was perfect, down to fountain pens on the desk beside dispatch boxes and an insurance policy on the house in the safe

King and his family in. There was truth in that, but George also actively preferred being squashed in the little house with its small rooms. When Alix died in the winter of 1925 there was no longer any excuse for them not to take over the big house.

The move to the Big House

'Very sad that tonight is the last night that we sleep in this dear little house in which we have spent 33 very happy years,' the King wrote, shortly after Alix's death in 1925. Queen Mary said too that she was reluctant to leave her 'very cosy and comfortable house'. But she was secretly relieved to be moving into the spacious big house, and devoted much time to reorganizing and decorating it without incurring her mother-in-law's disapproval.

The change of residence only served to enhance King George's role as squire of the Sandringham Estate. He paid his workers well and involved himself in the life of the community. He liked to tell of the time he helped a local boy with his maths homework. He offered to help again a few weeks later but the boy politely refused him. George wanted to know why, and the boy replied to his question uncomfortably, 'You got it wrong last time.'

👑 *A portrait of Queen Mary as she was at the beginnning of George's reign* left. *From the early years of their marriage George looked to her for comfort and support, which she never failed to give him all through his life*

George's relationship with David, his heir, was much more troubled. He was once heard to say, 'I pray to God that my eldest son will never marry and have children, and that nothing will come between Bertie and Lilibet and the throne.'

The first Christmas broadcast

In 1932 George instituted the practice of making a Christmas radio broadcast to the Empire. The brief message, which he wrote himself, ran, 'I speak now from my home and my heart to you all; to men and women so cut off by the snows, the desert or the sea that only voices out of the air can reach them; to those cut off from fuller life by blindness, sickness or infirmity, and to those who are celebrating this day with their children and their grandchildren – to all, to each, I wish a happy Christmas. God bless you.'

For the next three years George broadcast a message on Christmas Day in his slow, hoarse voice, to which his subjects listened while standing to attention. He found it an effort but prided himself on his performance. He would practise round the house for a day or two before, until his family and household knew his message off by heart.

These messages, delivered with such sincerity, added massively to his popularity. He took his role as King more seriously than anything and this communicated itself in his voice.

Still in love after 40 years

On the 20th anniversary of his succession to the throne, getting on for 40 years after their wedding, George was still writing sincere, loving notes to his wife. 'I can never sufficiently express my deep gratitude to you, darling May, for the way you have helped and stood by me in these difficult times,' he wrote. 'This is not sentimental rubbish, but what I really feel.'

The Silver Jubilee

By 1935 George had been on the throne for 25 years and it was time to celebrate his Silver Jubilee. In his modest way he had never realized how high he stood in the hearts and estimation of his people, but the celebrations surrounding the anniversary left him in no doubt. The King was unhappy about the amount the festivities were going to cost and would have preferred no fuss, but in this he was overruled.

He was moved by the spontaneous show of affection from the crowds outside the Palace. At one point he turned, choked with emotion,

👑 *An ecstatic reception greets the King and Queen as they drive through the streets of the East End* above *during the Jubilee month of May 1935. The tremendous displays of affection during this time overwhelmed the King, for he had never realized how much the public respected and adored him and his Queen*

👑 *The day marking King George's Silver Jubilee began with a beautiful service of thanksgiving at St Paul's Cathedral* right. *Later that day, in between repeated balcony appearances, lunch and dinner, George broadcast his Jubilee message to the people*

to May. 'I had no idea they felt like that about me,' he said. 'I'm beginning to think they must really like me for myself.'

He also spoke of his bemusement to the Archbishop of Canterbury. 'I'm sure I can't understand it,' he said. 'For after all, I am only a very ordinary fellow.'

A popular monarch

It was his ordinariness as much as his Royal dignity that made him popular. He was under no illusions about his own talents. 'I am not a clever man,' he once said, 'but if I had not picked up something from all the brains I've met, I would be an idiot.'

He was convinced that the cheering was as much for May as for himself. In one of his Jubilee speeches his voice failed as he mentioned his feelings for her. 'I can't trust myself to speak of the Queen when I think of all I owe her,' was all he could say.

The King was now infirm. He had nearly died in 1928 when he contracted bronchial pneumonia, and he had never been fully well since. A narrowing of the arteries to his brain meant that he would suddenly fall asleep, sometimes at meals. He used to have a night nurse to administer oxygen to him when necessary.

But duty and routine kept him going. Every morning his breakfast companion was Charlotte, a grey and yellow parrot who travelled with him almost everywhere. She was allowed to roam about the table, taking pecks at whatever she fancied. He would cover any mess she made with a napkin in the hope that Queen Mary wouldn't notice. Then at 9.30 he would speak to his sister, Princess Victoria, on the phone. Her greeting to him was always: 'Hello, you old fool!' He liked telling the story of how she had once gaily shouted this as she picked up the phone, only to hear the Buckingham Palace operator on the other end say with embarrassment, 'Beg pardon, Your Royal Highness, His Majesty is not yet on the line.'

Overcome with grief

Their close relationship had survived even her feud with his beloved wife, so he was devastated when she died on 3 December 1935. Not even the death of his father, mother or son had affected him as this did. For the first time ever he cancelled the State Opening of Parliament.

As usual, the family spent Christmas in Sandringham, but the King was weak with illness and grief. A few days later, Dawson, the Royal physician, arrived.

Soon afterwards, George lapsed into a coma which lasted two days. On the evening of Monday 20 January, Dawson released a simple bulletin: 'The King's life is moving peacefully to its close.'

> ## 'I can never sufficiently express my deep gratitude to you, darling May, for the way you have helped and stood by me'
>
> GEORGE

A street in southeast London is decked out in flags on the occasion of King George's Silver Jubilee above. While the Jubilee celebrations extended to all areas of the city, it seemed that the King and Queen received their most enthusiastic welcomes in the poorer districts of the East End of London

Popperfoto

By gracious permission of HM the Queen

♛ 'Mary R and Baby Elizabeth' *below*. Queen Mary photographed in 1927 with her granddaughter, Princess Elizabeth of York, who was to become heir to the throne nine years later when her uncle abdicated. Mary doted on Elizabeth from her birth, when she described her as 'a little darling'

TREASURED MEMORIES

THE PRIVATE YEARS

George and Mary saw the monarchy through some of Britain's most troubled years and they were unflinching in their dedication to the heavy task. Too rigidly brought up to be able to discuss their feelings, the couple had early discovered that they could express their deep and vital love for each other in writing. The tender letters continued until the day George died, but it was during those years of comparative obscurity that together they forged the strength which would enable George to take up the crown and Mary to bear her widowhood

Mary R
Baby Elizabeth
1927

♛ *Above* King George with his doomed youngest child, Prince John, in 1911. John's epilepsy was getting very much worse at this time and he and his nurse, Lala Bill, moved to the more peaceful Wood Farm, about two miles away on the Sandringham estate

♛ *Above* Mary with the tiny boys who would both be King. Four-year-old David *(right)* already shows the impish charm which captured the nation's heart when he became Prince of Wales, while Bertie (left) seems to be practising for future solemnity

♛ *Right* A charmingly informal photograph of Mary taken in 1897, during the tranquil years of domesticity at York Cottage

♛ The delight of George's declining years and probably the bane of Mary's, Charlotte the parrot *below* lived in the King's bedroom and was there when he died. Charles Cust, George's equerry, was the only person who dared to complain about her breakfast table antics when she dug her beak into his boiled egg

WIDOW AND MATRIARCH

**QUEEN MARY FACED HER WIDOWHOOD WITH FORTITUDE AND A
CALM RESOLUTION, DETERMINED AS ALWAYS TO BE OF SERVICE TO
HER COUNTRY AND HER FAMILY**

The papers break the sad news inset right. Almost a million people filed past George's coffin during the four days of lying in state at Westminster Hall right; the crowds who came to bid the King farewell on his last journey below were so vast they blocked the processional way

GEORGE V DIED AT 11.55 PM ON 20 January 1936 with his family gathered round him. Without a word or cry, Mary immediately turned to the new King. 'My mother did an unexpected thing,' David, now Edward VIII, wrote later in wonderment. 'She took my hand in hers and kissed it; before I could stop him my Brother George, who was standing beside her, stepped forward and followed her example.'

The funeral procession from King's Cross to Westminster consisted of a gun-carriage followed by the new King and his three brothers on foot. The Imperial Crown was secured to the lid of the coffin, but as the procession turned into New Palace Yard the jewelled Maltese cross on the top of the crown fell off into the gutter.

'A most terrible omen,' Harold Nicolson wrote in his diary, and so it seemed to be. On 16 November 1936, the new King went to dinner with his mother to talk about his love for the American divorcée, Mrs Simpson. Queen Mary was distressed and sympathetic – until David made it clear that he was going to marry Mrs Simpson, even though it would mean renouncing the throne. She could not imagine that anyone could put personal preoccupations above duty, least of all her own son, the King.

Further strain for Mary

The strain of the abdication coming on top of her husband's death made Queen Mary ill. She could not eat and during the crisis lost 25 pounds in weight. Her second son, the Duke of York, now destined to take his brother's place as King, also needed her support.

But it was not in Queen Mary's nature to go into a decline. The new King needed her support, and she needed to be well enough to give it. With effort she pulled herself together, and her obdurate courage was much admired. Her personal popularity was at a high during George VI's Coronation, and a machine on a roof in Whitehall measuring crowd noise during the procession showed that the coach carrying Queen Mary and her granddaughters received the loudest cheers of all.

When the worst of the mourning period was over a different side of Mary emerged.

Popperfoto

Daily Mirror

THE DAILY PICTURE   NEWSPAPER WITH THE LARGEST NET SALE

No. 10,028   TUESDAY, JANUARY 21, 1936   One Penny

THE KING DIES: HIS HAND CLASPED BY THE WEEPING QUEEN

Nation of Grieving Homes

THE "Daily Mirror" announces with the deepest regret that his Majesty King George V died last night at Sandringham. He was aged seventy.

THE FOLLOWING OFFICIAL BULLETIN WAS ISSUED JUST AFTER MIDNIGHT:—

"DEATH CAME PEACEFULLY TO THE KING AT 11.55 P.M. IN THE PRESENCE OF HER MAJESTY THE QUEEN, THE PRINCE OF WALES, THE DUKE OF YORK, THE PRINCESS ROYAL AND THE DUKE AND DUCHESS OF KENT.

SIGNED: FREDERIC WILLANS, STANLEY HEWETT, DAWSON OF PENN."

The Queen, with tears running down her cheeks, sat with the King's hand clasped in her own.

The King lay motionless in his bed. He made no sign of recognition to the other members of his family who were sharing the Queen's vigil.

As his life slowly ebbed away he passed into a deep coma.

When she realised the end had come, the Queen turned to her son—the new King—and mother and son exchanged an affectionate embrace. Edward Windsor, now Edward VIII of England, turned to his brothers and his sister with sad face, and the royal party moved slowly out of the death chamber.

Then the Queen, whose iron self-control had kept her calm through the long, anxious days, broke down.

The sad news was flashed to all parts of the world. The nation, sitting at its fireside, heard it over the wireless.

With the chimes of Big Ben as a majestic requiem, the King's passing was announced by the B.B.C. at 12.15 this morning.

For the first time, wireless had told a sorrowing kingdom of the passing of a British Sovereign.

Sir John Reith, director-general of the B.B.C., himself went to the microphone.

"It is with great sorrow," he said, "that we make the following announcement: His Majesty the King passed peacefully away at a few minutes before twelve."

Listeners in their homes, the crowds round Buckingham Palace and at Sandringham, knelt in silent prayer. Many wept. The King was at rest.

John Frost

THE ROYAL COLLECTOR

As she got older Queen Mary became very acquisitive. Often, awkwardly enough, she saw the very piece she longed to have in the homes of friends or even slight acquaintances. She had discovered years before that if she admired an object her hosts would often make her a gift of it. This became her favourite ploy.

If her flattering remarks produced no response she would go a stage further. She would stand in front of the piece and look at it longingly, saying slyly, 'I am caressing it with my eyes.' If that did not work, she would return to the subject again at the end of her visit, saying, for example, 'May I go back and say goodbye to that dear little cabinet?'

Hardened friends ignored even this, and Mary's final sally would be a letter of thanks with a request to buy the piece. Few were able to resist such a blunt demand, and would gracefully give in and give her what she wanted. She rarely had to pay

would like to perform the task, and passed the biscuit over. The bishop was rather deaf and, misunderstanding the gesture, thought he was being offered a delicacy it would be rude to refuse. He thanked her and dutifully ate his way through the hard, tasteless rusk, feeling unable to protest.

Queen Mary stared in horror, but it was too late to stop him. Sheer good breeding helped her control her laughter, but as soon as he left she wept with mirth.

'After the King's death ... all her great worth was revealed'

PRINCESS ALICE ON MARY

The Second World War

In 1939 war broke out and Queen Mary moved to Badminton, where she spent the entire six years with a retinue of 65 servants and staff. She was violently anti-German and anti-Nazi. As a fluent German speaker herself she was particularly displeased by the way Hitler spoke his native language, with an accent she thought was abominable.

Queen Mary was determined to do her bit for the war effort. She lived strictly on rations (as did all the Royal Family) and economized on hot water and washing by re-using the same napkins after meals. She scavenged the countryside looking for anything she thought might be useful towards war work. Any piece of metal left lying around in a field would be borne off

Her sister-in-law, Princess Alice, said, 'In her youth she was gay and amusing and would often be in fits of laughter. As Queen she was so sedate, so *posée*. But after the King's death she blossomed once more and all her great worth was revealed.'

Lady Airlie also vouched for the fact that Queen Mary was born with a great sense of humour that she had learned to stifle as unseemly. Before she was Queen, Lady Airlie said, 'I can remember her ... learning the words of "Yes we have no bananas" – the silly song hit – and singing it with me at the tops of our voices for the joy of shocking a particularly staid member of the Household.'

Mild eccentricities

It was not that George had repressed Mary's natural sense of humour, but that she herself had thought it was not fitting for a Queen Consort to behave in a certain way. Now that she was removed from the throne as a Queen Mother she saw no reason not to indulge herself in mild eccentricities and have a good laugh now and again.

One story she liked to relate concerned a bishop. It was a ritual that when she stayed with a certain niece she would give one of the dogs a dog biscuit after dinner.

One evening she graciously asked the local bishop who was dining with them whether he

☙ Below *A touchingly informal view of the grandmother who was 'the very symbol of the solidity of the British Monarchy'. Queen Mary casts a protective eye on the eight-year-old Prince Michael of Kent as the Royal Family watch King George VI return from Trooping the Colour on 8 June 1950*

Popperfoto

home by her. These often had to be secretly returned to their owners, as they were perfectly good farming implements which had been left out to be used the next day.

In 1942 her favourite son, the Duke of Kent, was killed in a flying accident. Once again, although she was personally devastated, she pulled herself through by making herself useful. She spent much time with the grieving widow, Princess Marina, helping her to put her life back together.

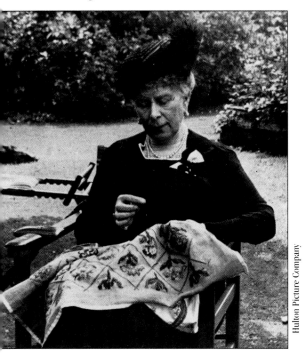

At the end of the war Queen Mary was coming up for 80, but still had plenty of energy to spare. She missed the seclusion of Badminton, and lamented that she would have to 'be Queen Mary again', but she soon regained her spirits. At one celebration, she and Lady Airlie joined in country dancing at Sandringham and didn't stop until past one in the morning.

She was delighted when her granddaughter, Princess Elizabeth, fell in love with Prince Philip. Although her son, George VI, thought his daughter was too young to marry, she supported the young couple in their plans.

The year Elizabeth and Philip married was also the year Queen Mary celebrated her 80th birthday. The Duke of Windsor flew over to be with his mother, though his wife was not invited. Crowds lined the route to Buckingham Palace, where a special birthday lunch was laid on, and so many people turned up to wish her well that mounted police had to clear a way.

She celebrated Elizabeth's wedding with the best of them. Two nights before the wedding day a large party was held. 'Saw many old friends,' she wrote in her diary. 'I stood from 9.30 till 12.15 am!! Not bad for 80.'

Prince Charles was born in 1948. To Queen Mary it was a very moving moment and much thought went into her gift: 'I gave the baby a silver gilt cup & cover which George III had given to a godson in 1780,' she wrote in her diary. 'So I gave a present from my gt grand-

👑 Above *The first great-grandchild. Mary holds the month-old Prince Charles in her arms just after his christening in the Music Room at Buckingham Palace*

👑 *Mary was an expert with her needle above right. In 1950 she presented the nation with a carpet which had taken eight years of work. It was to be sold to help buy dollars, as her contribution to solving the economic crisis*

👑 *Mary's Lady of the Bedchamber and life-long friend, Mabell, Countess of Airlie, is shown left expressing her opinions at the National Gallery, June 1945*

MARY AND HER GRANDDAUGHTERS

Mary enjoyed a much better relationship with her grandchildren, the Princesses Elizabeth (or 'Lilibet') and Margaret Rose, than she had with her own children. She was delighted that Lilibet, in whom she saw a resemblance to Queen Victoria, would one day be Queen, and Margaret simply enchanted her with her wicked charm.

Mary took it upon herself to help with the education of the little Princesses. Manners and duty were important aspects to her. On one occasion she was walking through Buckingham Palace with Lilibet when a courtier greeted the child familiarly. 'Good morning, little lady,' he said. 'I'm not a little lady, I'm Princess Elizabeth,' Lilibet retorted, walking on. Queen Mary called her back. 'This,' she said to the man, 'is *Princess Elizabeth* who hopes one day to be a *lady*.'

She also sought to convey to the girls her love of art. She took them to museums and art galleries, and lectured them on the great heritage which the Royal Family possessed. This she rather overdid. When Princess Margaret had her own children, her memories of hours trailing after Queen Mary had, she said, formed her belief that they should only be shown one or two fine paintings at a time, then be taken away while they still wanted to see more

---

father to my great grandson 168 years later.'

The last great tragedy of Queen Mary's life occurred at the beginning of 1952. Her son, his health broken by the heavy burden of Kingship, died prematurely after a short illness.

A new reign

Elizabeth was abroad when the sad news came. She arrived back at Clarence House on Thursday 7 February 1952. The old, grieving Queen Mary was the first of the family to be received by her. 'Her old granny and subject,' she said, 'must be the first to kiss her hand.' It was an emotional moment for both of them. Queen Mary had invested a lot of herself in Lilibet's upbringing and it shows. Queen Elizabeth II has plainly modelled herself more closely on her grandmother than her own mother.

Queen Mary felt too weak to attend her son's funeral. He was the fourth monarch and the third of her own sons she had to mourn. She stayed in Marlborough House with Lady Airlie and watched the procession from a window.

With her son's death she knew in her bones that she would not have much longer to live. She busied herself sorting out her possessions, so that when she died everything would be in good condition for her heirs. But there was still spirit left in the old lady. 'I am losing my memory but I mean to get it back,' she told a friend.

Queen Mary would have liked to have lived to see Elizabeth crowned Queen, although she knew it was unlikely. She stipulated that if she did die before the Coronation then mourning should not be allowed to modify it in anyway. She died on 24 March 1953. Her last outing had been to see the decorations for the Coronation of Queen Elizabeth II.

She was buried next to her beloved husband in the family vault in St George's Chapel, Windsor, on 31 March 1953.

Hers had been a life full of tragedy, not least having to survive her adored Georgie by nearly 20 years. But once when she was talking to the Queen Mother about the regrets in her life she said, 'There's one thing I never did and wish I had done.' Her daughter-in-law looked at her expectantly. 'I wish I had climbed over a fence,' Queen Mary said.

Below *Mary's upright, unchanging figure was a national emblem from 1893 to 1953, a period during which the rest of the world changed almost beyond recognition. In true royal tradition, she never spared herself in her determination to fulfil the role for which she had been born – a legacy the Royal Family retains*